# GATECRASHER

SUSAN BUIS

# GATECRASHER

## SUSAN BUIS

Invisible Publishing

Halifax & Picton

Library and Archives Canada Cataloguing in Publication

Title: Gatecrasher / Susan Buis.

Names: Buis, Susan, 1955- author.

Description: Poems

Identifiers:
Canadiana (print) 20190085487 | Canadiana (ebook) 20190085495
ISBN 9781988784267 (softcover) | ISBN 9781988784328 (HTML)

Classification: LCC PS8603.U528 G38 2019 | DDC C811/.6—dc23

Edited by Leigh Nash
Cover and interior design by Megan Fildes | Typeset in Laurentian
With thanks to type designer Rod McDonald

Printed and bound in Canada

Invisible Publishing | Halifax & Picton
www.invisiblepublishing.com

We acknowledge the support of the Canada Council for the Arts and the Ontario Arts Council.

Canada Council
for the Arts

Conseil des Arts
du Canada

ONTARIO ARTS COUNCIL
CONSEIL DES ARTS DE L'ONTARIO
an Ontario government agency
un organisme du gouvernement de l'Ontario

---

*To my family, with love.*

# SHELTER

Pero yo ya no soy yo,
Ni mi casa es ya mi casa.

But I am no longer I,
Nor is my house now my house.

— FEDERICO GARCÍA LORCA

## Arrowslit

Quarry the stuff of a curtain wall, quarry the crenellation.
And when a skirmish weathers, I'll lob projectiles—
rakes and broomsticks over firebreak stubble
like dragonflies buzzing ponds they left as nymphs.
Ghastly aqua larvae. An arrowslit's devoid of pane,
wide enough for side-eye, too narrow for full frontal,
a tenant in chamber backlit with petrochemical yellow—
archrival without rival.

More than neural zone, the gap is open to artillery
and eye both besieged and beseeching. I love the vertical
strip of it—miles and miles of kind of blue,
blue haze, blue train and all blues, miles of round midnight.
A missile hit to curtain wall jolts the humming switch box,
burns out beyond the breakers, their orange spot indicators
but not a pebble shuffles.

## Deconstructure

Amid tatters of the lowest bid,
a tenant posed in a higher floor's ruin
holds the tired arc of a story
as the epilogue volleys through.
They built tower block like human,
skin over conduit, rebar for sinew;
nerve bundles laid under cladding,
tense at the core, but swaying on impact.
Anointed with perfume, a room
became a home where headphones gave
sanctum from earshot combat, now gone
though ghosts of walls ring.
Clouds of sheetrock hold
as if they need not sigh over asphalt
and auto, nor hush the merciless
edges of tagged bins. In the lift shaft,
rags bandage white PVC pipes,
bones of the chariot down
broken with beams of night.

## Mud the cracks

We plan for shocks by fits and starts,
stockpile kits: water and batteries sure
to stale. Sugar for shock. Engineers draft
streets to skirt faults, line them with greens
and the torpor of flowers for ease.
We plan for damage, hoard patches, seals,
adhesives that brittle, then neglect
our stores. With repeat fractures,
repairs become the thing mended: ceiling
as cicatrix, massed hydrangea bracing
the split fence. Before the shaking,
crows screeching like metal-fatigued
planes will wake us.

## Vaxxer

Dreams of smashed ampules, after the attack—
the drone and pellets. Confess I stalked my own child,
overseer in a hot car watching
a string of five-year-olds walk to the lagoon
while I stewed with mistrust for their minders.

Dreams of rubble, the crushed bones
of freeway and concrete city,
me crawling over it like a spider, parents crawling
like spiders to find their children;

in the preschool yard, they'd wait, wrapped
in emergency kit blankets. Hold on
to your granola bars, your bottles of warm Dasani.
Children in silver foil.

Darling, I haunted you,
believed my arms were all you'd need,
wished for you the pox scar, this bloom
that parts us.

Dubrovnik: arms

In the span between fourth year and four square
meters of dispensary floor, I run through a stone
city from nothing to nowhere, through the span of
a costume change while soldiers—small gods smoking—
swap shirts brown as tobacco or honey, arms leaning
on a gimcrack Soviet jeep. The smell of cigarette
triggers the Istanbul market sweet with it, where
I bartered a rug rolled small enough to hold
under my arm, small enough to fit over the space
I will wear away with sensible shoes for thirty years.

I wear yellow for youth, flats that slap stone, skirt as
scant wrapping over a gift of hungry legs, run through
the city's armature of shell calcium whittled from
the coastline's chalk belt. Stolid Roman arcades brace
their flat feet, piggyback Gothic arches, arms pointing
to heaven as if to avert the siege that soon
will smash them. In a lull before the shelling, I run
through a white stone city.

## Roma: architectural drawing

Lick your pity, your buttery plate.
With appetite deckle-edged from exile
in a grey-stone province, bouquets
of salt blooms and rot up the overcoats, you flee
to slake it here with warmed glasses of light
yellow as good oil, yellow
as gilt and marbled ratios.

A swallow's-eye view holds the fortress plan,
its forced perspective upswept like a blown dress
showing ribs of path through green, navel
a fountain. Above, a black-eyed villa
rises to a sky edged in dark disorder.

Belvedere, beautiful sight,
how does your garden grid?
With golden means and triads of trees,
the arch of their crowns set with oranges,
with symmetry and the rich fruit of threes
and, at night, the blossoms.

## Costume

An adult hand drew the limbs, worried
more meals to the haunches, more fat
for the plate, contoured the cleft hoof
that signifies meat-giver. But the child's hand
curved a falcon's eye and domestic ear,
planted a heart on the forehead
red as cockscomb, and painted a striped hide.
For who, if given choice, would not want
to be motley? Pattern old as light
ribboned through stems, through eyelids
that weavers dreamed looms to mimic
with bands of pale horizons.
We suit up for pageants in bell, horn
and pelt—trust it takes just the slightest prop
to become beast.

## Constituents

An edifice so unyielding,
plumbed and laid in courses
as mortar fused the red-brick
school and civic block.

The new products give. Vinyl
covers the brief now—
in the interim earwigs bicker
and colonies of mildew bloom
their civilization
under its supple veneer.

A palm to masonry makes no impression,
perceives the wall's burden borne
though the fired weight limits height.

Accused were jailed down
here, spirits held cold in the cellar.
The intuitive see them looping
an action like hatchet or gavel
reeling prayers off their own tongues.

The ground pushes and eases
till bonds show crazing
in the zigzag—whispers of laity
fill the cracks.

Mud-red brick behind the eyes
red brick in the eyes
close your eyes, it's red brick you see
mud from luscious red beds.

## Knee play

From behind the heavy curtain—rustles
as the day is stitched into its costumes.
I rely on my ear to know the weather—
if I should wear blue or a sweater.

Trellis

You arrive through petal bloom and hoop
through passage wrought and twined.
How a clear muscle averts its clutch
like ash limb from obstacle.

Why lift tarnish off a structure
you're demolishing? Blue haloes
the nails and grain,
those gutters with crawling things.

Your path leads to the cellar,
its mushy cartons to heave,
litres of copper preservative
and apricot preserves.

The good-looking one will come (invited)
with clouds to shove beneath a pyre.
(His white teeth!)

## Shelter

A vault, frame or nest
holder of light and cries
conceptual, whimsical, not just physical:
a fine form of shelter.

Three small children hunker in a radial
of slim poles, gather under folds
of haphazard hessian: a makeshift shelter
just a skin away, just a skin away.

With daydreams of structure
no sense of how-to, no nail, no lumber
we settle for a lean-to, blanket over bushes:
a fine form of shelter.

A husband wields a chainsaw
carves the south-face casement
rotted to the rings' heart, spraying
bits of pine log: our fine form of shelter.

## 50s design

Mid-century wheels in a tea trolley—
blunt for progress and polished
to patina bright as a new economy,
bound to rust-freckle and squeak.
Its cursive frame, kin to trombone
balks at the stair, trembles on the incline,
can carry drinks but barely hold a tune.
The thirsty want modern ceramic, sans-serif cups
proxy for a tea service of bone china,
not from China, though from bone,
with the whiff of empire about it.
Precious little good now, ruined
by harsh devices that chore for us,
then carted off, crazed all over.

## Tarpaulins

We hoist our blue heavens and knot
far corners round trunks so scabbed
and black they might be charred,
folding chairs splayed under this slant firmament,
one part membrane one part wing:
a campers' Frank Gehry.

Sparks sail past the edge of our staked claim,
past Acadian mixed-wood canopy into a star atlas
shot with mica—not so bright as the strings
of LEDs that swag our tarps, nor moon so pleasing
as the orb of plastic cups pouring phosphor light.
Should clouds wobble in, crack like eggs and stream
albuminous rain, we trust our heavens will not fray
at the grommets, sag at the seams, or sluice glaucous
rivers through nylon beds.

## Knee play

Snow constant as tinnitus—
constant as a bilious gnaw—
hisses like carbonated drink,
like flux of waves on a coarse beach.

## Superb white-tailed buck

A felt presence nudges you
from a dream rut, and through glass a deer grins
as if caught in trespass, bared teeth
perfect and square as celebrities'.
Don't be fooled by grace that the animal
is benign—it hungers like the rest of us.
Its horsey bite could maul your lip—
did you feel the night peel you?
The muzzle sniffs, hankering salt—
is your dream sweat-crusted?
And craving, you've guzzled broth that burnt so
all the way down that still you're scalded.
The dark eyes seem warm,
though you misread glances,
your view sweetened by a waking pink.
Morning, tracks in snow tell a deer
did stand at the window, shuffled weight
as if restless, lifted its scut and shat pellets.

## Not a goat at all

Balance is a discipline. The rock I lean into—
discipline. Lacquered with ice it's tempting
to fear the face of it, but I have expert grip
and pant a warm atmosphere that muffles me.
Lose nerve and it deflates. The one about
how all love stories are ghost stories
stirs memory of a white goat
scaling a stone pitch as if floating
in the yellow prescience of autumn.
Its sure-footed poise just adaptation.
Birth luck.

The work of water wears rock
and soaks canals of dreams
my thought body—a perfect
vehicle—manoeuvers, though I wake fraught
and imperfect, all hinges whining.
The dream is like new ice, though, slippery
and melting. Me, scrabbling to maintain it.

## Oxen

Castrated placid, the pair holds a red yoke's
weight, red tassels lolling on muzzles.
Horned, yes, but tips sheathed.

Flightless Lark and Linnet
impassive in the face of a teamster's goad.
Hearts stud leather halters—such is human love.

## Osprey

For the dive, for the strike and clutch
muscles shiver in communion
to hold a hover through gusts
bending air to arc, wavering
a spread fan, wings tensile
as spring branches. In the gap
before the articulate plunge
all trembles but the eye
fixed on a brackish creek upwelling
with sweet eels that thrive
in briny confluence and streaks
of red weed swaying in the gullet—
weed that's weft for a scavenged
wood warp, mass of nest
to weave another stick through.

# Beetle song 1

You laugh, it reminds us of denuded
we slide a pine serif
blind in sweetness

phloem tide, hum down tune
eat thick rubric

the wound is endless
ambient pressure squeezes
a crevice moon

purple crave, purple crave
purple crave, purple crave

pressure curls a Persian gazelle
loops and strings of pearls
over the milty way

saline sheen squeeze between
tillers, murmurous clandestine

Sappers (beetle song 2)

We cross the viridian
chased by smoke
so lie low, burrow

vers sigh
carve up the palace
from south to north crown

looting galleries
we spoon-scrape and eat cake
the veins' rosy marrow

sappers undermine the brittle sky
peel back veneer
famish the caches

hot light scalds
where we smash through
resinous red heaven

saboteurs lay charges
along hewn corridors
blue tripwires will bring it down

Lucky cat

Flanked by consorts of toy robots birthed
through vending machine slots
calico cat paw-pumps blessing
on a realm of stacks and foldings:
a three-storey walkup, no bath, but a roof
overhead or someone's floor, anyway.
In the flat's dusk a butterfly large
as two spread hands, beacon in a gift shop frame
reflects light incident and indigo
from scaled wings. Blue morpho
beat through its lifespan alternating dun
with iridescence. My own pounding
heart I've seen flaring in a sonogram's frame.

## Eating goat on Capricorn's birthday

To my hunger, I move rice
and fingers of whisky; to the question,
I give my sign but know not my house,
my rising. Deadpan diner windows,
the North Shore behind, flashing
its tail and twitching. Seems always dark
now, but here's a lamp for our sun,
a white cloth for our drippings.

The young have ordered goat
with a round of praise for its gravy,
lift cubes to square teeth, bare
arms ringed in seasonal glitter,
eyes gold beeswax, for this meal's just
prelude to night's burning.

At work today, a colleague told the tale
of the swan that bends to slit its breast,
for blood to nourish fledglings
as the young lean in to take it.

## Mutt

In the rear-view oval a furred hill
waxes in a glass sky; though gripping
the wheel, my palm flashes with impulse
to pet the eloquent crest.
Dog's got my back.
Coeval, we stretched to latch,
hand adapting to cup wolf's crown
as skull to meet it pulled.
With gesture old as want, we're
heliotropic to the other's sun.
Inhale, her coat licks of meal fat
and held petrichor. Exhale,
the curve's in me.

## Knee play

A few laundered things ping
the bathtub thin as the keel of a cheap
boat that needs bailing, where I soap
off shallots and other lingering alliums.

## Schemering

Dusk, we cycle a trail gone intuitive.
A chill under pink-limbed trees, spectral stones
and brush all washed in woad.
Imprimatura pulls this canvas together. Undershadows
soak everything: a penumbral stain through entrails
(robin's egg and iris, a surgeon told you), the hiss
of the wheels' slide, axels lubed with blue-black grease.
Blue in spoke, in rubber, chrome, aluminum.
You leave grip of a handlebar, stroke
the seeded skin of the field. Blue in that, too.

## Highlands

Forests hewn and hauled
or glacier scraped like spade on rock;
many acts of clearance
bear many states of desert.

We tramp a bitter heave of land;
the straps of our necessities
vex us. Wayworn over distance,
our puny shanks rise from lace-ups
stout as hooves of dray horses.
You've seen to proper raiment with fetish
for gear. (Twenty backpacks I found
in the shed, your hoard of latent journeys,
twenty buckled longings.)

A forest should leave some trace;
a few pines, scouts or remnants
struggle in the leas, like striplings
hard put in bald pastures struggle
through easterlies, though nurtured
with rations of greywater:
Nursery trees, such thin surrogates.

## Talewort

Common borage, talewort, fuzzy as moth to thwart
consumers—still, we sprinkle it on foraged greens,
lore gathered in wicker. For a walk alone with you, July,
our skins pinto under softwoods. The blue star's
cardiac tonic, locals say, as if a flower could…
as if a heart could…

Let's stay in touch, you write, though I'm slow to decipher
the script, seldom reading cursive now.

Yet it's in her handwriting that Dickinson's poems quicken
to me, stride to the turn and evade, though room bound
slinging dashes to rend just a glimpse.

# Theatre

Tug the pin and a drowsy pall
settles like moths blurring
the liminal between your perfect shadow
and the fill spot. The house coughs, rustles.
Garish at close quarter, greasepaint improves
over distance, is striking even.

Exit stage door, pull night's wool
tight and grass disappears underfoot.
Anonymous, so fervid, you open
to the greater metropolitan, its glazing
split by power lines and tonight's lunar transit.
Soot scatters a ruddy spectrum,
stains the moon's disc manganese,
your lips' occlusion lurid.

### Knee play

Pollen has made of the glass door a thing—
beyond, green plastic chairs on the balcony
have been conversing for three weeks
but seem no closer to an understanding.

## Scullery

The kitchen is catchment for breakage,
a pine and tile corral
and though I've not fallen to this
floor, what's cast down shatters: a mat
of ceramic, facets of quartz, me
with buttery hands absent of task
lost out the window's enchantment.

We make meaning in tandem.
I sweep shards, listen hard, lyricist waiting
for partner's tune. Your string
of words pearls to ellipsis... for me
to draw our exquisite corpse.

January

Slant winter sits out with me in short sleeves,
warm and companionable, silent as a poised heron.

We've had no music for years, but feed on fat
in broth—pints and pints of it—beaded with oil
yellow as the eyes of birds, and in yolks near peach
specked with pinches of ground sea.

Expat and thrifty, I skimp my measures.
Corn can be gleaned, and molluscs
with their gritty, explicit bodies. Seaward
of waterline, no one's claim, is my harvest.
But lack whittles affection, belts
loosed and slipping.

You need look up at me

Trust the material economy
of fabric, invest in future gains.
Our clothing allots tucks
and easement, while drafts are kept
of smaller selves, betrayed in picked-out
stitches and creases like waterlines
no amount of steam will erase.
Some balk at unalterable acts done
without thought or want: the prickle
of thickening and splitting,
the frightening appetites of adults.
The bone ache of it. And the patient,
accompanying acts of scissors and needle.

## Celadon

Solenoid, he must have said, head under hood
but I hear celadon, imagine a green-glazed dish
glowing in the Ford's leaden perplexity: a pale
stopped heart that won't give a charge.

He takes the wheel. I shove the beater's stern
to find a current east towards the darkening,
shove to hear the blessed click and cough
when the engine flips. The lane's colonnade
of elms hiss as they inhale dusk
after a July day's hot pounding. Body cocked—
an ear pressed to night's humming screen: cicadas
courting in code, a wrestle of bats, the diminishing
mutter of the car. Departure a reprieve
for at least one of us.

## Knee play

Slips away—an oiled thing—
flicker in a cephalopod's lantern. Thick
air will loosen, precipitate its cast eye.

## All in all

Apologies skirt the quarry
shy like cattle before wading
into its clear green pool.
There's no hurry, apologies wait
in the heat's brief season. Some
never learned to dive, split the water
splayed, kick at the surface
piping like frogs. Some
swallow their pit fears, breach
security on the limestone cliff
and leap into the deep end
with its banquet
of livestock carcasses
stolen cars and fruit
of other crimes.

## Bridge

A fretless bass measures a good sleep, but lately
I surface in the caesursae to see how far
I've come. The stuff of the world is slurry,

a runny alchemy fluxing the ceiling vault—
so gold I lift through it, rehearsing
a small death.

Once, I lived a winter month over water, bath
draining to pool unnoticed below cellar trapdoor;
I was not sensitive to it. High spring found awash.

At the river's mouth, a seal with dog face and dog eyes
rides a lace of oil on the swells: seer watching
a poor swimmer dip down the troughs.

The losses

*Lose something every day.*
— ELIZABETH BISHOP

All this rain. Knuckles thicken, click.
Pinky a crooked little piggy bent as a fib.
Inflammation's a bad song on heavy rotation.

Pert left with suckle. Resign
to holes, or lumps in the grey mush.
Auntie warns: don't be a garden
swelling to bolt.

Your retriever won't fetch
the name of that white-flowered
weed with silver leaves.

The small motor runs longer—
little bitch outliving great hound.
Sure, time saves mercy for the heart's pain
and pearls it—the process oiled
in its susurration.

If romance is longing
for one out of reach, then you're in thrall
with your lost sylph, little silk
underthings now poor dust cloths.

## The injuries

The tip of a cigarette, point of an antler,
open palm and steel apparatus.
Homebody, recluse, a nun in burnt ochre.
Trespass on ranch land, draw glass architecture.
Smoke stinks of plastic, of ozone and glycerine,
campfire, camphor, musk and gun cotton.
Air sweet with ions, and rivers with chlorophyll,
chloroform. You're accessory, complicit,
are witness or innocent.
Sing doctrine to Bartók, believe in the system,
believe honeyed rhetoric, in fate,
that it's random. Sew up wounds
with thread dipped in whisky, wounds licked
by insects, or open and blistered.
Utter silence, the pad of a cat, slip
of a Swede saw, glance of axe,
blade of red laser, scalpel of grass.

Plead drugs from physicians, files thick
and sealed, files in ribbons. Clinics are ransacked,
empty and shuttered; sentries lead dogs
round perimeter fences.
Call for grandmother, sister, for pilot or clergy.
Children feral, lost in camps, isolated in suburbs.
Bear nightshade, death angel, great felt skirt,
shadows on X-ray, darling dirt.

# ROSE HILL

## Yank

I yank Brassica, scourge a field by hand,
pull clumps of shrill yellow that bees shun
for sweeter landings.

Road crews lustred in glyphosate sweat
nozzle Roundup—its loose ways
with boundaries. Over stake and rail
direct stream and easterlies serve
a broad-spectrum desiccant, smolder a tan strip
where voles and tumbleweed root.

So I mow a preemptive belt, tilt
at invasives with a Craftsman 190cc.
On suburban lawns, this tool is
king, but on ranchland it's a paltry thing
wielded till it chokes and
I clear the clogged maw, eyes effervescent,
sting of mustard on the septum.

Pollen!

I'm green to the cell, weeding barehanded
and split-nailed. A wetter spring pushes pollen
in peppered gusts to sneeze—
how many tiny muscles wrenched?
Fertilization is fruit of the irritant;
oleasters' yellow clouds gild nostrils and eye-rim red.
Burgundy fescue and blue rye heads'
tiny jewels and spiked maces commit
millions of tiny violences to tender places.
My gaze is greased and fevered,
lungs sour with grassy water that seeps.
Wind delivers my dose of snuff,
a rural cut.

## Kejimkujik dark sky preserve

Around the Sky Circle, tourists' cells
slant to capture the thick wrap of galaxy,
flares cycling the platform like some guttering-out
midway ride. Our weak irises fumble
with things of the world soaked in wild dark,
though truest black's
reserved for the teeth of hemlock
ringing the lake's jaw, light sliding
off spikes sharp as cries.

On Rose Hill, concerned residents upgrade
yard lamps for thousand-lumen
floods over outbuildings, washing out fields
where we would lie, stargazers
under flight paths, cast from our point of uncoiling
to heaven's sprung ribbon.
All above and in.

The blaze of our transactions,
our failure to douse towers,
dim night with settlement's glow
even to bed, where holding novels we drowse
in incandescent shallows.

Olives

Ten kilos of fresh olives, a knife,
hours to slit each twice to speed
the leaching. With Buñuel's razor
slicing a woman's eye
in mind, I wince at each give,
though I know the bleached
face of a dead calf
was held in the zoom. Still—
the gush over her lashes.

Olives green as the chlorophyll glare
of the feral cat— though I can touch her
now, run the wild nerve of her spine.

Two weeks sluiced in a creek works best
to rinse the bitter from the fruit
but it's a dry year. I opt
for brine, yet am ungenerous—
the efforts of my curing, spat.

## Half-lit morning of the longest night

The wind sounds dry, I hear grit. Strung out
lights swinging one length blown. Whiskeyjack
shows what's broken, though I already know,
my annoyance static fur. Thanks
for the no-show. The out-of-whack
radio slips its channel, sails the bandwidth
B-100 to The River. I'll ring you later.
In the archives of the prosaic, I wipe
coughed-up snippets of things pets can't digest;
outside, things of the world don frost pelts.
Glints of gravel in a raven's throat
rattle challenge to the red-tail he pesters.

Day stalks the pasture's fringe.
Beyond, a neighbour with lantern checks
a herd carrying curves of spring. Beam
to fodder, to black sides of cattle,
her ancient act of husbandry.

Summer, your limbs moved like the new rope
and pulley of the laundry line, to let the staring sky
work for a bit.

To town

In a state of low alarm, faith held
in suspension through degrees of grade
and bands of cloud, maneuvering a machine on ice
an act of nerve and good rubber, cortisol
churning the low gut like a virus. My hands jitter
when I reach work from the weight I've navigated
through the long vertical glaze to the lot, its grid of lines
and my spot among them, fear riding bitch
through twelve Ks of down. I've seen it
all go sideways on the stretch: rollovers,
plastic florals lashed to a pole, once a flipped van
in flames—a woman running to it
with a blanket. A blanket.

## Settle

The starling thicket ticks—
neurotic, neurotic's no mantra.
Invasives nickel in their swiveling blades,
thrive along the septic,
sucker twigs snipped and talling to
the eaves, where the ladder
has ascended since flickers drilled
a hole to patch and rot has tendered grey.
Oleasters hold the starlings'
settle, they lift, regather a new compression.
I'd murmur rue, but have no confessor.
Here for now, we've landed—
our clutter over everything.

## Grassland pointillism

Plate glass patted down by foundling cats,
little mutant goons born under outbuildings,
swatting at moths left a veil of eight-toed mitts
up the pane. I see brassy flies have been at it too,
spattered the window with a thousand points of shit.
Deeper of field, buzzed metal hills roll, specked
with those Black Angus spared fall's stockyard cull.

Untended roses brush the glass, petals browning
at edge. A plucky late flowering.
Flocked with blight, weevil-punctured leaves
sift wood smoke—burning still permitted
here, outside the limits. Floaters dot the eyes,
swim over gold-flecked Formica holding
sheets of Schubert Lieder: rows of black notes
the house singer will run into a stream of sad love.

## The air will take it through an hour

Forty Celsius, I put a pan of water in the sapling's lee
for birds, least weasels, and feral cats. Even insects
come to sip. This summer the nursery hawthorn
is hardy enough to lay a mat of shade, host to
a flurry of blackbirds.

Curtains drawn against the sun's unregulated glare,
on grey gauze an avian shadow play:
oily black wings strobe white,
leached like silver negatives,
an eye migraine's pangs of light
cut with the *scree* of cicadas.

Elephant Hill fire

Smoke slips between northern shield and northern lights
smooth as the knife that loves its passage.
We live within this immanent smolder
till we're habituated to it,
to the drone of aircraft hefting
loads of water to waterless sky
while yarrow bolts to brown,
smoke moving like a thick spill
dumbing us as we go through our motions.

Another burnt-yellow dawn peppered with unlocked
carbon from the forest's mouth, coughed
into our mouths. Prep for going:
gather cat cage and husband's pills,
tap shots of rooms to prove our worth—
assets viewed later found abject,
all of it fodder.

## Laid up

How just like that
a drone's-eye view has replaced the bird's
flyover of a burned-out town through a birdless sky.
Music and injury swell,
subside.
Give me good reason to rise:
Previcox for dog,
water for nursery trees—also limping.
Varietals bred for gentler zones
persist in failure to thrive.
Even through all this smoke, the glint
of a galvanized pail sharp as thirst.

## Gatecrasher

Maybe only one slipped through—
masked in mucky feed, or a horse trailer
stowaway from god knows where.

Its burred offspring thrives in dirt
sapped by the scrape and whack
of former tenants who carved

their names in concrete, staked
kennels on spent soil, milled cash
from dog flesh—mounds of thirsty pups

in a hot skinny pen. The weed's
absent from guidebooks: local
and far afield. Unchecked

it's a mass of flower fireworks—radiant
Catherine wheels and blue bursts—
a flourish that parches with its guzzle.

As I rip armfuls of garlands
loosed seeds shower like sequins. I sow
as I pluck and spade.

Even sleep is specked with unblinking
blue-bead eyes: dream flowers
slim legged and spurred

with stars that prick gloves, socks,
and stud the dog's wool.
We become carriers,

like the scalpel a friend suspected
seeded healthy tissue and quickened
the spread, told me this

without bitterness or blame—
just wanted, she said, for wisdom
to understand—

yet there's no reading of it, no
cunning, only growth so fecund
that all around it withers.
I'll take her unclaimed anger
to augment mine.

Offering

After cattle are trucked from lease lands, I walk
the bunchgrass zone in orange hoodie
to deter hunters. Already this season—

incidents. Tossed shot-shells and Bud cans
glitter at the hem of our settlement. Beyond
is trespass, and resource economy,

and this morning in fall's brown half-life, another
ditched mule deer carcass. When what's wanted
is taken, the remainder is heaved

for scavenge. But this doe
is recomposed with something like care
severed shanks crossed on bowed head, hide

folded to bare a blue-white fascia
as if the animal held winter inside its very skin.
Crows' ha has! puncture the low-slung sky.

How neatly a body can be parcelled—
bound in red the hue of drugstore
lipstick that shows me sallow.

## Respite

Beauty hangs from a limb at night,
swaying over the crawling grass
and burrows. Oleaster roots
fracture green stone
to flush silver leaves and pill sour fruit
that only blackbirds can stomach,
plumed in oil and beet.

I hang beauty to sway in boughs
charged with blackbirds' racket
of rat squeals and weird gold
eyes. Night leaves its burrows
to crawl through the grass,
while I rest, relieved
of weight.

## Observatory

O the universe is leaking, porous.
Space junk pricks heaven and galaxies
run out.

Bubbles pop in the ointment,
and in ice melting in sweaty glasses
by our beds—

you in Venice over night-lapped pilings, me
on our Rose Hill bed hiked up
with bricks, both moon-pulled and damp

in early, rude heat. I ooze salt
under the fan's squeaky orbit,
sucking stray words into its slipstream

as mouth to ear—no, to a silver cell,
my voice in your canal. Look,
beyond our weeping fields, across the road:
Angus cows calve great black progeny
into the strawdust, their ripped, wet
membranes coyote feast.

And yesterday, the new dog, hit by a gas truck,
her stove-in body a pierced fur sac.

The stellar pelt
I stroked—the night, the stars—
seeped pink through a blanket on the vet's
concrete floor.

In our pantry, the liver, a treat I bought her,
bloats warm and ignored, strains
the strings of its paper packet.

## South window

The end of February is rot
without resurrection: moth-holed sky
over Rose Hill Road buckled
from cartage and salt, woodpile
exhausted to dregs, compost
choked with husks and rinds:
mouthfuls of winter's grounds.
Starving owls are gristle and faint;
this desert's glaze of ice shields voles
bunkered in their fur-lined runnels
and shitty little nests.
                              The snowy owl
drowsing on the utility pole will take
any drunken mouse that staggers
from the compost's core or,
at worst, a thin meal culled
from the chipping sparrows that shelter
on the casement, so trusting
then startled by your movement
behind their own cocked reflections.

THANKS

I offer heartfelt thanks to poets Pete Smith, Deanna Young, Adèle Barclay ("Pollen!") for their wisdom and advice. My warm gratitude to Leigh Nash for her patient, meticulous editing. Love to dear Shauna Caicco, Susan Cline, and Karen Hofmann for bringing poetry to my life.

And thank you to the fine people at Invisible Publishing for their enthusiasm and positive energy.

## NOTES

"All in all" appeared in *Contemporary Verse 2* as "apologies"

"Costume" appeared in *Poetry Is Dead*

"Gatecrasher" appeared in *Another Dysfunctional Cancer Poem Anthology*

"South window"
appeared in *The Fiddlehead*

"Superb white tailed buck"
appeared in *Vallum*

Versions of "Arrowslit," "Osprey," "Scullery" were longlisted for the 2016 CBC Poetry Prize within the suite *architectures*

Knee plays are brief "joints" connecting theatrical acts, performed in front of the curtain while sets and costumes are changed

"Not a goat at all" is indebted to "The Limits of What We Can Do" by Natalie Eilbert

"Beetle song 1" and "Sappers (beetle song 2)" are for artist Ernie Kroeger and Pablo Neruda's "Sonnet LI"

A selection of these poems won the 2017 John Lent Poetry/Prose Award (Kalamalka Press) as the collection *Sugar For Shock*

INVISIBLE PUBLISHING produces fine Canadian literature for those who enjoy such things. As an independent, not-for-profit publisher, our work includes building communities that sustain and encourage engaging, literary, and current writing.

Invisible Publishing has been in operation for over a decade. We released our first fiction titles in the spring of 2007, and our catalogue has come to include works of graphic fiction and non-fiction, pop culture biographies, experimental poetry, and prose.

We are committed to publishing diverse voices and experiences. In acknowledging historical and systemic barriers, and the limits of our existing catalogue, we strongly encourage LGBTQ2SIA+, Indigenous, and writers of colour to submit their work.

Invisible Publishing is also home to the Bibliophonic series of music books and the Throwback series of CanLit reissues.

If you'd like to know more please get in touch:
info@invisiblepublishing.com

Invisible